HAL•LEONARD
INSTRUMENTAL PLAY-ALONG

AUDIO
ACCESS
INCLUDED

PLAYBACK+
Speed • Pitch • Balance • Loop

CELLO

CONTEMPORARY BROADWAY

Audio arrangements by Peter Deneff

To access audio, visit:
www.halleonard.com/mylibrary
Enter Code
5851-4797-0032-8660

ISBN 978-1-5400-5934-5

HAL•LEONARD®

Visit Hal Leonard Online at
www.halleonard.com

Contact us:
Hal Leonard
7777 West Bluemound Road
Milwaukee, WI 53213
Email: info@halleonard.com

In Europe, contact:
Hal Leonard Europe Limited
42 Wigmore Street
Marylebone, London, W1U 2RN
Email: info@halleonardeurope.com

In Australia, contact:
Hal Leonard Australia Pty. Ltd.
4 Lentara Court
Cheltenham, Victoria, 3192 Australia
Email: info@halleonard.com.au

CONTENTS

ALL THAT MATTERS

from FINDING NEVERLAND

CELLO

Words and Music by ELIOT KENNEDY
and GARY BARLOW

DEFYING GRAVITY
from the Broadway Musical WICKED

CELLO

Music and Lyrics by
STEPHEN SCHWARTZ

Allegro, as before

Slower

ME AND THE SKY

from COME FROM AWAY

Cello

Music and Lyrics by IRENE SANKOFF
and DAVID HEIN

Country Folk

MICHAEL IN THE BATHROOM

from BE MORE CHILL

CELLO

Words and Music by
JOE ICONIS

rit.

Slower

mf

accel.

To Coda ⊕

D.S. al Coda

a tempo

CODA
⊕

f

mf

MY SHOT
from HAMILTON

CELLO

Words and Music by LIN-MANUEL MIRANDA
with ALBERT JOHNSON, KEJUAN WALIEK MUCHITA,
OSTON HARVEY, JR., ROGER TROUTMAN,
CHRISTOPHER WALLACE

ONCE UPON A DECEMBER
from the Broadway Musical ANASTASIA

CELLO

Words and Music by LYNN AHRENS
and STEPHEN FLAHERTY

PRACTICALLY PERFECT

from MARY POPPINS

Cello

Music by GEORGE STILES
Lyrics by ANTHONY DREWE

PROUD OF YOUR BOY

from ALADDIN

CELLO

Music by ALAN MENKEN
Lyrics by HOWARD ASHMAN

Moderately slow

Orch.

RIGHT HAND MAN
from SOMETHING ROTTEN!

CELLO

Words and Music by WAYNE KIRKPATRICK
and KAREY KIRKPATRICK

SEIZE THE DAY
from NEWSIES THE MUSICAL

CELLO

Music by ALAN MENKEN
Lyrics by JACK FELDMAN

Faster

SHE USED TO BE MINE
from WAITRESS

CELLO

Words and Music by
SARA BAREILLES

STUPID WITH LOVE

from MEAN GIRLS

CELLO

Words by NELL BENJAMIN
Music by JEFFREY RICHMOND

D.S. al Coda

CODA

WAVING THROUGH A WINDOW
from DEAR EVAN HANSEN

CELLO

Music and Lyrics by BENJ PASEK
and JUSTIN PAUL

CODA

WHEN I GROW UP
from MATILDA

CELLO

Words and Music by
TIM MINCHIN

WHERE DID THE ROCK GO?

from SCHOOL OF ROCK

CELLO

Music by ANDREW LLOYD WEBBER
Lyrics by GLENN SLATER

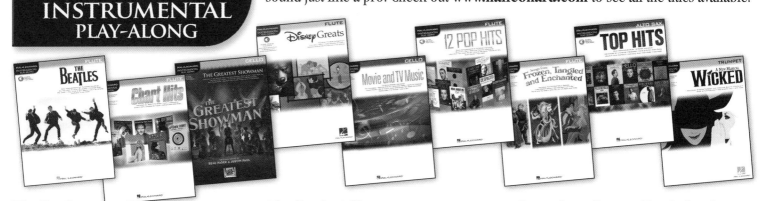

HAL•LEONARD INSTRUMENTAL PLAY-ALONG

Your favorite songs are arranged just for solo instrumentalists with this outstanding series. Each book includes great full-accompaniment play-along audio so you can sound just like a pro! Check out **www.halleonard.com** to see all the titles available.

The Beatles

All You Need Is Love • Blackbird • Day Tripper • Eleanor Rigby • Get Back • Here, There and Everywhere • Hey Jude • I Will • Let It Be • Lucy in the Sky with Diamonds • Ob-La-Di, Ob-La-Da • Penny Lane • Something • Ticket to Ride • Yesterday.

____	00225330	Flute	$14.99
____	00225331	Clarinet	$14.99
____	00225332	Alto Sax	$14.99
____	00225333	Tenor Sax	$14.99
____	00225334	Trumpet	$14.99
____	00225335	Horn	$14.99
____	00225336	Trombone	$14.99
____	00225337	Violin	$14.99
____	00225338	Viola	$14.99
____	00225339	Cello	$14.99

Chart Hits

All About That Bass • All of Me • Happy • Radioactive • Roar • Say Something • Shake It Off • A Sky Full of Stars • Someone like You • Stay with Me • Thinking Out Loud • Uptown Funk.

____	00146207	Flute	$12.99
____	00146208	Clarinet	$12.99
____	00146209	Alto Sax	$12.99
____	00146210	Tenor Sax	$12.99
____	00146211	Trumpet	$12.99
____	00146212	Horn	$12.99
____	00146213	Trombone	$12.99
____	00146214	Violin	$12.99
____	00146215	Viola	$12.99
____	00146216	Cello	$12.99

Disney Greats

Arabian Nights • Hawaiian Roller Coaster Ride • It's a Small World • Look Through My Eyes • Yo Ho (A Pirate's Life for Me) • and more.

____	00841934	Flute	$12.99
____	00841935	Clarinet	$12.99
____	00841936	Alto Sax	$12.99
____	00841937	Tenor Sax	$12.95
____	00841938	Trumpet	$12.99
____	00841939	Horn	$12.99
____	00841940	Trombone	$12.99
____	00841941	Violin	$12.99
____	00841942	Viola	$12.99
____	00841943	Cello	$12.99
____	00842078	Oboe	$12.99

The Greatest Showman

Come Alive • From Now On • The Greatest Show • A Million Dreams • Never Enough • The Other Side • Rewrite the Stars • This Is Me • Tightrope.

____	00277389	Flute	$14.99
____	00277390	Clarinet	$14.99
____	00277391	Alto Sax	$14.99
____	00277392	Tenor Sax	$14.99
____	00277393	Trumpet	$14.99
____	00277394	Horn	$14.99
____	00277395	Trombone	$14.99
____	00277396	Violin	$14.99
____	00277397	Viola	$14.99
____	00277398	Cello	$14.99

Movie and TV Music

The Avengers • Doctor Who XI • Downton Abbey • Game of Thrones • Guardians of the Galaxy • Hawaii Five-O • Married Life • Rey's Theme (from *Star Wars: The Force Awakens*) • The X-Files • and more.

____	00261807	Flute	$12.99
____	00261808	Clarinet	$12.99
____	00261809	Alto Sax	$12.99
____	00261810	Tenor Sax	$12.99
____	00261811	Trumpet	$12.99
____	00261812	Horn	$12.99
____	00261813	Trombone	$12.99
____	00261814	Violin	$12.99
____	00261815	Viola	$12.99
____	00261816	Cello	$12.99

12 Pop Hits

Believer • Can't Stop the Feeling • Despacito • It Ain't Me • Look What You Made Me Do • Million Reasons • Perfect • Send My Love (To Your New Lover) • Shape of You • Slow Hands • Too Good at Goodbyes • What About Us.

____	00261790	Flute	$12.99
____	00261791	Clarinet	$12.99
____	00261792	Alto Sax	$12.99
____	00261793	Tenor Sax	$12.99
____	00261794	Trumpet	$12.99
____	00261795	Horn	$12.99
____	00261796	Trombone	$12.99
____	00261797	Violin	$12.99
____	00261798	Viola	$12.99
____	00261799	Cello	$12.99

Songs from Frozen, Tangled and Enchanted

Do You Want to Build a Snowman? • For the First Time in Forever • Happy Working Song • I See the Light • In Summer • Let It Go • Mother Knows Best • That's How You Know • True Love's First Kiss • When Will My Life Begin • and more.

____	00126921	Flute	$14.99
____	00126922	Clarinet	$14.99
____	00126923	Alto Sax	$14.99
____	00126924	Tenor Sax	$14.99
____	00126925	Trumpet	$14.99
____	00126926	Horn	$14.99
____	00126927	Trombone	$14.99
____	00126928	Violin	$14.99
____	00126929	Viola	$14.99
____	00126930	Cello	$14.99

Top Hits

Adventure of a Lifetime • Budapest • Die a Happy Man • Ex's & Oh's • Fight Song • Hello • Let It Go • Love Yourself • One Call Away • Pillowtalk • Stitches • Writing's on the Wall.

____	00171073	Flute	$12.99
____	00171074	Clarinet	$12.99
____	00171075	Alto Sax	$12.99
____	00171106	Tenor Sax	$12.99
____	00171107	Trumpet	$12.99
____	00171108	Horn	$12.99
____	00171109	Trombone	$12.99
____	00171110	Violin	$12.99
____	00171111	Viola	$12.99
____	00171112	Cello	$12.99

Wicked

As Long As You're Mine • Dancing Through Life • Defying Gravity • For Good • I'm Not That Girl • Popular • The Wizard and I • and more.

____	00842236	Flute	$12.99
____	00842237	Clarinet	$12.99
____	00842238	Alto Saxophone	$12.99
____	00842239	Tenor Saxophone	$11.95
____	00842240	Trumpet	$12.99
____	00842241	Horn	$12.99
____	00842242	Trombone	$12.99
____	00842243	Violin	$12.99
____	00842244	Viola	$12.99
____	00842245	Cello	$12.99

HAL•LEONARD®